MAKE YOUR OWN
COMEDY

by Jonathan Quijano

Consultant:
Tad Kershner
Founder
Montalto Visual

CAPSTONE PRESS
a capstone imprint

Velocity is published by Capstone Press,
1710 Roe Crest Drive, North Mankato, Minnesota 56003.
www.capstonepub.com

Books published by Capstone Press are manufactured with paper
containing at least 10 percent post-consumer waste.

Library of Congress Cataloging-in-Publication Data
Quijano, Jonathan.
Make your own comedy / by Jonathan Quijano.
p. cm. -- (Velocity: make your movie)
Summary: "Provides instructions for how to make your own comedy movie"--Provided
by publisher.
Includes bibliographical references and index.
Includes webliography.
ISBN 978-1-4296-7530-7 (library binding)
1. Comedy films--Production and direction--Juvenile literature. I. Title.
PN1995.9.C55Q55 2012
791.43'617--dc23   2011029439

Editorial Credits

Editor: Lisa Owings   Media Researcher: Emily Temple
Designer: Marie Tupy   Editorial Director: Patricia Stockland

Photo Credits
Capstone Studio/Karon Dubke, cover; Shutterstock Images, cover (background), 4, 37
(bottom); Everett Collection, 5, 25, 37 (top); Mary Evans/Paramount Pictures and Fox
Searchlight/Ronald Grant/Everett Collection, 6; Paramount/Everett Collection, 7, 8
(bottom), 36; 20th Century Fox Film Corp./Everett Collection, 8 (top); Warner Brothers/
Everett Collection, 9, 19 (bottom left); Brian Chase/Bigstock, 10; Rick Becker-Leckrone/
Bigstock, 13; Jacqueline Perez/Bigstock, 15; Jon Quijano/Red Line Editorial, 16; Rick
Orndorf, 18, 23, 28, 29 (all), 30 (all), 31, 34, 43, 44; New Line Cinema/Everett Collection,
19 (top), 32; Mary Evans/Python Pictures/Ronald Grant/Everett Collection, 19 (bottom
right); Mykola Velychko/Bigstock, 21 (top); Red Line Editorial, 21 (bottom), 26;
iStockphoto, 27; Nina Matyszczak/Bigstock, 33; Fox Searchlight/Everett Collection, 38;
Marc Dietrich/Bigstock, 39; Yuri Arcurs/Shutterstock Images, 41; Dana Rothstein/
Bigstock, 45

Printed in the United States of America in Stevens Point, Wisconsin.
102011   006404WZS12

HA
HA HA

TABLE of CONTENTS

Introduction to COMEDIES

HA HA HA

You will have a blast making your own hilarious comedy film. This book will help you make your audience laugh until it hurts. Get ready to tap into your inner comedian!

Many beginning filmmakers make comedies because they cost little to make. You can make a great comedy without costly or time-consuming special effects. All you need is good writing, funny actors, and a little bit of imagination!

MISMATCHED ELEMENTS

Combining mismatched elements can make people laugh. For example, *Elf* (2003) is a comedy about a human raised as an elf. It is funny because of how out of place the main character is in both the elf world and the human world.

THE SCIENCE OF LAUGHTER

Comedy is about making people laugh. Scientists have studied what causes people to laugh. They have noticed a few things:

We laugh at things that don't match. A big, tough-looking man who talks with a tiny, high-pitched voice is funny.

We laugh at surprises. For example, a person sleepwalking would be a little bit funny. A person sleepwalking into a neighbor's house, eating food from their fridge, and ending up asleep in their bed would be funnier because it is less expected.

We laugh when we feel superior. Charlie Chaplin was a comedian who starred in silent films throughout the early 1900s. Chaplin got a lot of laughs because he made clumsy mistakes.

In *The Circus* (1928), Chaplin accidentally locked himself in a lion's cage.

TYPES OF COMEDY

PHYSICAL / SLAPSTICK

Features:

- main character is unlucky or clumsy
- funny accidents involve falls and other comic pain
- silly violence with cartoonish sound effects, such as a bonk to the head combined with a hollow clunk
- exaggerated movement

Examples: *Christmas Vacation (1989), Napoleon Dynamite (2004), The Pink Panther (2006)*

BUDDY

Features:

- two main characters with opposite personalities
- characters dislike each other but become friends by the end
- characters work together to achieve a goal

Examples: *Tommy Boy* (1995), *Blades of Glory* (2007), *The Other Guys* (2010)

SPOOF

Features:

- mimics a well-known movie or movie **genre**
- sometimes has exaggerated costumes
- **deadpan** humor

Examples: *Monty Python and the Holy Grail (1975), Airplane! (1980), Robin Hood: Men in Tights (1993)*

HA HA HA

SATIRE

Features:

- **Satires** make fun of common faults in people or society.
- rebellious heroes who break the rules

Examples: *Wayne's World (1992), Mean Girls (2004), Hairspray (2007)*

MOCKUMENTARY

Features:

o   shot in the style of a documentary

Examples: *Drop Dead Gorgeous* **(1999),** *Best In Show* **(2000),**
A Mighty Wind **(2003)**

genre—a category of art characterized by
similarities in form, style, or subject matter

deadpan—describes humor delivered with
a serious voice or facial expression and a
matter-of-fact style

satire—mocking humor used to show how
foolish or misguided someone or something is

BEFORE THE SHOOT

You won't get any laughs by being unprepared for your movie shoot. Plan every detail of your shoot during preproduction.

Writing Comedy

The first step in writing a comedy is to come up with a comical story. Here are some ideas to get you started:

- **Keep a dream journal.** Get in the habit of writing down your dreams as soon as you wake up. Funny dreams can give you strange and silly ideas you would not have thought of otherwise.

- **Watch lots of comedy.** Watch as many comedy movies as you can. Take notes on what makes you laugh. Then figure out how it made you laugh. Was it the way an actor said a line? Was it the timing of when they spoke it? The more you learn about how other comedies work, the funnier your own movies will be.

- **Think about something funny that happened to you or to a friend.** People love to share funny stories, so keep your ears open for good ones. Maybe you or a friend had an embarrassing experience that would make a funny scene.

Three-Act Structure

Any good comedy needs three main parts: a beginning, a middle, and an end. In movies and plays, these parts are called acts.

ACT 1

- The main character's funny or odd personality gets them into trouble.
- The main character has to figure out how to get out of trouble. The main character's plan is often hilariously outrageous.

ACT 2

- The main character's personality makes it hard for her or him to get out of trouble.
- The main character gets a second chance.

ACT 3

- The main character tries out a new plan.
- The main character either succeeds or fails. Most modern comedies have happy endings to keep the mood light.

HA HA HA

Creating Funny Characters

Comedy comes from unexpected situations. Funny characters don't do or say what people expect. For example, you would expect to see someone walking a dog around the block. But you wouldn't expect to see someone walking a hamster. Imagine watching someone try to walk a rabbit! Give your comedic characters unusual interests and personalities. These traits will get them into funny and unexpected situations.

Exercise

Make a list of people's unique appearances or habits. These could include:

- family members who stay true to themselves no matter what other people think
- teachers who have unusual behaviors
- people you see in public who behave or dress oddly

Make notes about these people. What makes them stand out to you? What about their behaviors and personalities make them funny to you?

Exercise

Many comedy writers make the mistake of creating characters that aren't fully developed. Get to know your characters by answering personality questions about them.

Think of what your character would say to these questions:

- What do you like most and least about yourself?
- What is your favorite childhood memory?
- What was your most embarrassing moment?
- What is your deepest fear?

Writing Funny Dialogue

As in every kind of movie, **dialogue** in comedies has to tell the audience what is happening in the story. But comedies have a greater challenge than most other movies. The dialogue also has to be funny.

Eavesdrop

Go to places where plenty of conversations are happening, such as restaurants, parks, or shopping malls. Bring a notebook. Secretly listen to what other people are saying to each other. Write down funny things that might work as dialogue in your movie. Take notes not only on *what* funny things people say, but also on *how* they say them. Listen to people's tone of voice, watch for body language, and pay attention to timing. This will help you develop your ear for comedic dialogue.

dialogue—a conversation between two or more characters

Build to a Punch Line

Most dialogue in a comedy builds toward a punch line. This dialogue is called the setup. A punch line is the line that delivers the joke.

Example from *Monty Python and the Holy Grail* (1975)

SETUP {
Father: You only killed the bride's father, that's all!

Launcelot: Well, I really didn't mean to.

Father: Didn't mean to? You put your sword right through his head!

Launcelot: Oh, dear. Is he all right?

PUNCH LINE

TIP Write what you know. Most comedy writers draw from their own life experiences. Nia Vardalos was the writer and star of *My Big Fat Greek Wedding* (2002). She was inspired by memories of growing up in a mixture of Greek and American cultures.

It's Funnier If the Audience Knows Something a Character Doesn't

Perhaps your main character falls asleep while studying. The doorbell rings and wakes him up. He doesn't know that he has messy hair, pen marks on his face, and drool at the corner of his mouth. He also doesn't know that his crush is at the door.

The scene is funny because the audience knows something the character doesn't. They know he is about to answer the door and look silly in front of his crush. The scene is also funny because it makes the audience feel superior to the main character. This technique works in many situations.

Exercise

Play with word choice to make things sound funnier. Think of an idea. Then try to come up with the funniest word to represent that idea. For example, say your idea is "city." Is "Indianapolis" funny? Is "Sheboygan" funnier? Brainstorm a funny food, pet, video game, or job title. Write down everything that comes into your mind, no matter what. The more often you brainstorm, the more funny words you will come up with!

Write Your Script

```
EXT. COUNTY FAIR DUNKING GAME — NIGHT

CLIFF sits on a platform over a tank of water.

JACOB walks up, pays a dollar to the VENDOR, and picks up a
ball.

Cliff points at Jacob.

                    CLIFF
              (shouting smugly)
         There is no way you can hit that bull's-eye!

                    JACOB
         We'll see about that!

Jacob throws the ball and misses the target.

                    CLIFF
              (laughing rudely)
         See? I knew you didn't have a chance!

Cliff laughs so hard that he loses his balance and falls
into the tank of water anyway.

                    JACOB
              (laughing)
         I guess you were right!
```

Once you come up with ideas for your story, characters, and dialogue, it's time to write your **script**. The dialogue in the script is especially important in comedy movies. Since a great deal of comedy is in what characters say, comedy scripts usually have more dialogue than other types of movies.

You may need to revise your comedy dialogue. Don't worry if the lines you had planned don't seem as funny when your actors perform them. Scripts aren't set in stone. You can change the dialogue in your script until you are happy with it, even while shooting.

Try organizing your script like the professionals do. Scripts are organized this way to make them easy to understand.

HEADINGS

- Start each scene with a heading that includes the place and time in which the scene is set. Use DAY for daytime scenes and NIGHT for evening and nighttime scenes. Use INT. (interior) or EXT. (exterior) to show whether the scene takes place indoors or outside. Make a new heading each time you move to a different place.

DESCRIPTION

- Describe the action throughout the scene. What are the characters doing? What actions, gestures, or situations will make the audience laugh?

- Describe the sights and sounds in each scene. What are the characters seeing, hearing, and reacting to? What funny details can you include in the scene?

DIALOGUE

- Show who is speaking by writing the speaker's name in capital letters above each character's line.

- Write your characters' dialogue. It is usually best to let your actors decide how to deliver their lines. However, you can include instructions in parentheses if needed. This may help actors deliver their lines in a funny way.

script—the written text of a movie

Finding Cast and Crew

Recruit friends and family to act in your movie. Look for people who like to perform and are naturally funny. If they don't want to act in your movie, ask them to be part of your crew.

You can also use people with funny talents. Can your sister walk on her hands? Maybe you can work that into a scene or two! Is your friend down the street a world champion belcher? Well, sign him up! If you can't find enough funny cast members, hold auditions.

Costumes and Props

Costumes for a Spoof Comedy

The challenge: imitating costumes from another movie

Your resources:

- **Halloween shops** sell costumes from the latest popular movies. These costumes are usually cheesy, which is good for making fun of whatever you are spoofing. They also stock classic costumes.

- **Costume shops** have a wider variety of costumes and props than Halloween shops. However, limit what you rent—it can get expensive! Also, plan to shoot your scenes quickly. You only get the costumes for a short time, usually a weekend.

- **Thrift stores or garage sales.** You can find hilarious costumes for cheap if you are willing to dig around.

Costumes for a Slapstick Comedy

The challenge: getting your actors to look cartoon-like

Step 1: Think Big

In *The Mask*, oversize clothing gave the illusion that the actors were larger.

Step 2: Crazy Hairstyles

Create crazy hairstyles with lots of hair cement. Ace Ventura, from *Ace Ventura: Pet Detective* (1994), had a hairdo that went with his larger-than-life personality.

Step 3: Bright Colors

Bright colors are cartoonish. Just wearing a Hawaiian print shirt will help.

The Mask (1994)

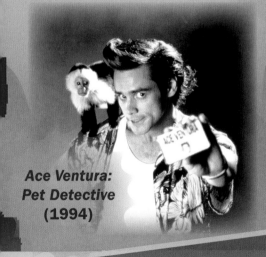

Ace Ventura: Pet Detective (1994)

A Creative Solution

The makers of *Monty Python and the Holy Grail* (1975) could not afford horses for their spoof about King Arthur's knights. They came up with a hilarious solution—they had the actors pretend to ride horses. A servant followed each character clicking coconut shells to make the sound of a galloping horse. The simplest, silliest solution ended up being the funniest.

Hold a Read-Through

When you're ready to start filming, hold a read-through. At a read-through, you meet with the actors and have them read the entire script. This gives the actors a chance to see how their parts fit into the movie. The read-through is also a chance for you to plan how you will direct and film each scene. Take notes as the actors read. What do you like about how the actors deliver their lines? What don't you like? Where will you place the camera for each scene?

HA HA HA

Improvise

At some point during the read-through, ask each of your actors to get in character. Talk to them and ask them questions. Have them **improvise** their answers. Tell them to say things their characters would say. Don't worry about everything being funny. Just keep going. This is a good way to help actors gain confidence in their roles.

improvise—to make something up on short notice

TIP Hold the read-through at your house or somewhere quiet and private.

Make a Production Schedule

Most movies are shot out of order. To stay organized, make a list of where and when each scene needs to be shot. Also list the characters and props you need for each scene. Group together all scenes that need to be shot in the same place and at the same time. Use your list to make a production schedule for your shoot.

A Sample Production Schedule

Date	Sets	Day/Night	Characters	Scene Numbers
Fri., May 1 Morning	Int. Chocolate Factory	Day	The Kid The Professor	4, 5, 10
Fri., May 1 Evening	Kid's House	Night	The Kid The Dad The Mom	1, 3, 7
Sat., May 2 Morning	Toy Store	Day	The Kid The Kid's Friend	2, 6, 8
Sat., May 2 Evening	Int. Jail	Day	Officer O'Malley The Kid The Professor	9

Lights, Camera, Action!

Now that you've planned every aspect of your shoot, you are ready to start filming. You will shoot all of the scenes for your movie during the production phase. The production phase of a comedy shoot should be fun and flexible. You may find that the shots you planned during preproduction don't seem as funny when you put them into action. Don't be afraid to make changes. Try a few different things and film the one you can't stop laughing about!

Directing Tips

1. **If you aren't laughing, it's not funny.** You are your own best judge. Keep trying different things until a joke gets you to laugh honestly. Use questions to get actors to try new things: "What if you used a more serious tone?"

2. **Keep quiet!** You should often feel like laughing out loud in the middle of filming a scene. But if you laugh out loud, it might spoil the shot. If you feel the urge to laugh, cover your mouth and keep it to yourself.

3. **Get the pace right.** Often a faster pace is funnier, but you still need to give the audience time to react to each joke. When filming a comedy scene, use your own reactions to judge how the audience will react to the pace. Guide your actors accordingly.

Improvisation

The funniest lines in a comedy are often not written in the script. The actors come up with them on the spot. If you have quick-witted actors, let them "improv" the scene. Have them invent their own dialogue with the camera rolling. Your actors may surprise you. Go with the flow, and have fun!

How to Use Improv in a Scene

With a single actor:

Simply point the camera at the actor and start rolling. Let the single actor improvise the scene as many times as he or she wants to. Keep the camera rolling no matter what. Later, you can choose the funniest takes and delete the rest.

With multiple actors:

In a scene with multiple actors, it helps to talk about the scene before shooting it. That way, the actors understand how they need to work together during the scene. They can still make up exactly what they will say and do once the camera starts rolling.

TIP

Once a group of actors has worked together for a while, improv becomes easier. The actors will learn each other's comedic styles and figure out how to play off one another to get the funniest result.

The Improv Rut

Not everyone is good at or comfortable with improv. Even if your actors are good at improv, sometimes they might get stuck in a rut. And that's OK! Here are some things you can do when your improv scenes aren't going as planned:

- Try something completely different. Changing up a scene can jump-start your actors' creativity.

- Remind your actors not to think too hard about what they will say next. Let them know that it's OK if they say something that isn't funny. Give them continuous encouragement to boost their confidence.

- Come back to the scene another day.

- Going back to the script will always be an option.

Whose Line Is It Anyway?
(1998–2006)
was a comedy TV game show
based on improvisation.

Lighting

If you film indoors, it may be too dark to clearly see the actors. Seeing actors clearly is especially important in comedy. Actors rely on facial expressions and body movement to make audiences laugh. Use lamps from your home to add extra light. You can also try using shop bulbs from a hardware store.

1. The Key Light

The key light is the main light on your subject. It is the brightest light, and it casts the darkest shadows.

2. The Fill Light

The fill light is a secondary light. It lightens the shadows created by the key light.

3. The Back Light

The back light shines from behind your subject. It helps set your actor apart from the background.

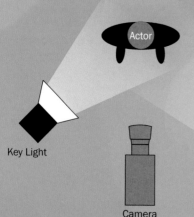

Back Light

Actor

Key Light

Camera

Fill Light

Experiment with changing the number, placement, and brightness of your lights until you get the effect you want.

Camerawork

Keep your comedy camerawork simple. Too much camera movement will distract from the funny people in the scene.

Finding a Camera

You don't need an expensive camera to make a good comedy. The audience will be focused on the characters, jokes, and the creativity of your story. If you have a home video camera, shoot with that. You can also rent a higher-quality video camera. But even the video function on your still camera or cell phone would work.

Try setting your camera on a tripod and leaving it motionless for each shot. Let the actors and your writing take center stage.

Some comedies do rely on camera technique. Most mockumentaries are shot with handheld cameras to mimic documentaries.

HA HA HA

Shoot for Editing

Try to get all of the following shots when you are filming. They are the building blocks you will use to create a scene. Shoot several **takes** of each shot. Later, you can create a scene using the funniest parts of each take.

ESTABLISHING SHOT

An establishing shot shows the building or area where the scene is taking place. Use it at the beginning of a scene to orient the audience.

MASTER SHOT

A master shot shows all of the actors performing the entire scene. The master shot is the foundation of your scene. Show as much of this shot as you want. Cut to close-ups to show details such as facial expressions.

MEDIUM SHOTS AND CLOSE-UPS

Get a variety of shots of all your actors during each scene. A close-up brings special attention to a specific detail in a scene.

Medium Shot (MS): shows the actor from above the knee

Close-Up (CU): shows the actor's head and shoulders

Extreme Close-Up (XCU): shows only a small part of an actor or object in the scene

take—footage from one continuous camera run

29

Reaction Shots

Show each actor's response to jokes, other actors, or events. Funny reaction shots sometimes get as many laughs as the dialogue, joke, or other part intended to be funny.

Visual Humor

Sight Gags

You can make people laugh without saying a word. A sight gag is a visual joke that doesn't depend on words.

Sight gags have to be very silly to get noticed. They work best in silly kinds of comedy. A slapstick comedy is a great place to use sight gags.

Elf (2003) filmmakers used sight gags to show that the main character didn't fit in with his surroundings.

PHYSICAL COMEDY

Physical comedy is another form of visual humor. It is also called slapstick comedy. In physical comedy, the humor comes from actors moving in funny ways.

This actor uses comedic body language in response to a very loud polka band.

Physical Comedy Effects

Pratfall

The **pratfall** is a very popular kind of physical comedy. Use a mattress to safely catch your actor as he or she falls.

1. Film an establishing shot of a person walking. Show the actor from head to toe.

2. Film a shot of the actor from the waist up. This time, have the mattress on the ground, out of the camera's view.

3. The actor should suddenly trip and fall out of view. Don't follow the actor with the camera. The actor will land on the hidden mattress.

pratfall—falling down for comic effect

TIP

Hide the mattress behind other objects in the scene.

Walk into a Glass Door

An actor is walking toward the camera. Suddenly, he or she runs into a glass door! This trick will surprise the audience, who may not notice the glass before the actor runs into it.

Two things sell this trick:

1. Out of view of the camera, the actor kicks the glass. This creates the "thud" sound at the moment of impact.

2. The actor's head snaps backward just short of hitting the glass. The timing of this reaction sells the trick.

   Set the camera up on one side of a sliding glass door. Be sure the glass is spotless and that there is no glare to give the joke away.

   Have the actor walk toward the camera, into the door.

The Rule of Three

An old rule in comedy is the rule of three:

1. Set up the joke.
2. Reinforce the setup.
3. Deliver a surprise as the punch line.

The rule of three makes us laugh because the second step sets up a pattern. The third step breaks the pattern and surprises the audience.

Rule of Three Example:

1. A man opens one closet to look for something. It's empty.
2. The man opens a second closet. It's empty.
3. The man opens a third closet. It's actually a bathroom. The bathroom is occupied.

The surprise occurs on the third step. Many jokes have this rhythm. Look for ways to use it in your own comedy.

AFTER THE SHOOT

Editing

Most computers have basic movie editing programs. They let you edit the best parts of your movie footage and assemble them into finished scenes.

A scene from *The Naked Gun* uses editing to deliver a surprise joke. A gunfight erupts in a factory. The hero and villain take cover. They shoot at each other from their hiding places. The editor cuts to a shot of the hero firing from behind his cover. Next comes a shot of the villain firing from his hiding place. But the editing of this scene has been hiding a trick. The audience finally sees the joke in the **payoff shot**. It shows the men were taking cover just a few inches away from each other!

The Naked Gun
(1988)

payoff shot—a shot revealing a joke set up by the previous shots

Comedy Sound Effects

During production, your focus should be on recording the actors' dialogue. In postproduction, editing programs let you add additional sound effects. These added sound effects are called Foley.

Slapstick comedies make great use of sound effects. The Three Stooges were popular characters in short slapstick comedy films throughout the mid-1900s. They were constantly beating each other up. Every punch and poke was emphasized by a funny sound effect.

The Three Stooges

With some simple musical instruments, you can make classic comedy sound effects. Most computers have built-in microphones and sound recording programs. Use them to record the following:

Pinch on the Nose
bicycle horn

Bop to the Head
hit a wood block
with a stick

Slipping on Ice
slide whistle

Music

Add to your funny movie with a **score**. Good comedy movie music is usually fun and upbeat. Pop music is popular. Happy-sounding music will put the audience in a good mood. In a good mood, an audience will find it easier to laugh.

Juno (2007)

score—the music accompanying a movie

SCORING YOUR MOVIE

1. Edit your film with no music added.

2. Keep notes on what kind of music you want, where you want it, and how long it should play.

3. If you're recording the music yourself, record the music while watching the movie play.

Where to Get Your Score

♪ Write and record the music yourself.

♪ Have a musically talented friend or family member write and record music for you.

♪ Buy recordings online. You can also look for royalty-free music, which you can use without paying a fee.

Comedy Focus Groups

You are almost at the finish line. The movie is written, shot, and edited. It seems pretty funny to you.

But comedy is a very challenging art form. It's hard to predict what will make audiences laugh. At this stage, arrange a focus group. Focus groups are groups of volunteers who watch the movie and say what they liked and disliked about it.

To hold a focus group for your comedy:

1. Invite three or four people to your house. Choose people whose opinions you trust. Let them watch the finished movie.

2. Write down what parts made them laugh. Also note any time they didn't have the reaction you were hoping for.

3. After the movie, ask them questions about the movie:

> What was your favorite part?
>
> What parts disappointed you?
>
> Who was your favorite character?
>
> If you could change one thing, what would it be?

4. Take notes on their responses.

5. Make changes to your movie based on your notes. Remember that you don't have to change something you like just because someone else had a different opinion.

If some parts of your movie fail to get laughs, you have some options.

1. **Re-edit for timing.** In comedy, pacing is everything. Do the actors tell their jokes too quickly and move on before the audience can laugh? Does a gag take too long to get to the punch line?

2. **Write a new scene to replace the old scene.** This means you will have to get the actors back, along with your costumes and camera equipment. Be sure this is absolutely necessary.

3. **Delete the scene.** This is very common, even with big-time Hollywood comedies. If your not-so-funny scene is a minor part of the story, leave it out. You may have to remove small parts of other scenes if they refer to the deleted scene.

 TIP Keep your deleted scenes saved in your computer. If you make a DVD of your movie, put the deleted scenes in a special features menu. Many people like to see what was left out.

YOUR PREMIERE

By now, you know that making a comedy is no joke!

Now comes the real fun. After your focus group, you should be confident in sharing your hilarious comedy with the world. It's time to give your movie its premiere!

Where to Show Your Movie

You can show your comedy film in a few different ways:

Public Premiere

Show off your movie the old-fashioned way by premiering it for a public crowd. You can show your movie at any of the following places:

- Small local theaters are often available for rent.
- School and library auditoriums may be available to reserve.

Private Showing

Your home is a great place to premiere your movie. Invite a small group and entertain them with your new comedy. You can show your movie on a projection screen or on your living room television.

Film Festival

Enter your comedy in a local film festival. Check with your local arts board to learn about film festivals near you. It's a great way to show your movie to new people, and you may win an award!

Comedy Web Sites

Maybe your comedy will be the next movie to gain popularity on the Internet. Post your movie on sites like YouTube for your friends and the public to see. There are even Web sites dedicated to comedy.

How to Make Your Private Premiere a Success

1. One month before your premiere date, send invitations to your family, friends, and everyone who helped make your movie.

2. Plan a short speech introducing your movie and thanking your team.

3. Serve refreshments and snacks after the movie. Be prepared to answer questions.

4. Give your audience response cards to fill out. Ask them what they liked and didn't like about your movie. You may be able to use their feedback to improve films you make in the future.

Build a Fan Base

Show your movie as many times and in as many places as you can. This will help you build a fan base. Then create a mailing list to keep fans informed and help promote your movies.

- Bring a sign-up form to every movie showing. Encourage people to sign up if they like your movie.

- The form should ask for a name and e-mail address.

- Each time you schedule a showing of a movie, alert your fans with an e-mail.

- Include the date, time, location, and directions in the e-mail.

Everyone on your e-mail list likes the movies you make. Use the list to advertise each new movie you come out with. This will bring your biggest fans back for more laughs. It also encourages you to continue making movies!

What's next? It's up to you!
See you on the next shoot!

GLOSSARY

deadpan (DED-pan)—describes humor delivered with a serious voice or facial expression and a matter-of-fact style

dialogue (DYE-uh-lawg)—a conversation between two or more characters

genre (ZHAHN-ruh)—a category of art characterized by similarities in form, style, or subject matter

improvise (IM-pruh-vize)—to make something up on short notice

payoff shot (PAY-off SHAHT)—a shot revealing a joke set up by the previous shots

pratfall (PRAT-fahl)—falling down for comic effect

satire (SAT-ire)—mocking humor used to show how foolish or misguided someone or something is

score (SKOR)—the music accompanying a movie

script (SKRIPT)—the written text of a movie

take (TAYK)—footage from one continuous camera run

READ MORE

Fleischman, Sid. *Sir Charlie Chaplin: The Funniest Man in the World.* New York: Greenwillow Books, 2010.

Grabham, Tim, et. al. *Movie Maker.* Somerville, Mass.: Candlewick Press, 2010.

Lanier, Troy, and Clay Nichols. *Filmmaking for Teens: Pulling Off Your Shorts.* Studio City, Cal.: Michael Wiese Productions, 2010.

INTERNET SITES

FactHound offers a safe, fun way to find Internet sites related to this book. All of the sites on FactHound have been researched by our staff.

Here's all you do:

Visit *www.facthound.com*

Type in this code: 9781429675307

INDEX